**The Impact of
Science and Technology**

TRANSPORT

Joseph Harris

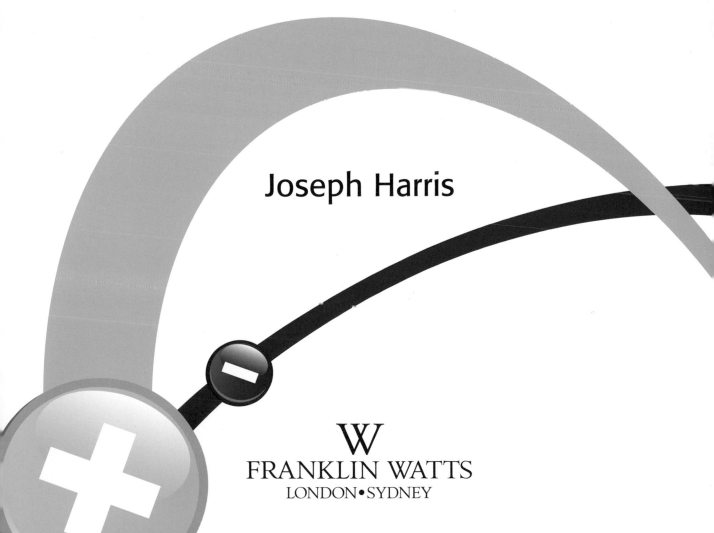

W
FRANKLIN WATTS
LONDON•SYDNEY

First published in 2009 by Franklin Watts

Copyright © 2009 Arcturus Publishing Limited

Franklin Watts
338 Euston Road
London NW1 3BH

Franklin Watts Australia
Level 17/207 Kent Street
Sydney, NSW 2000

Produced by Arcturus Publishing Limited
26/27 Bickels Yard
151-153 Bermondsey Street
London SE1 3HA

Series concept: Alex Woolf
Editor and picture researcher: Nicola Barber
Cover design & illustration: Phipps Design
Consultant: Miles Hudson

A CIP catalogue record for this book is available
from the British Library.

Dewey Decimal Classification Number: 388

ISBN 978 0 7496 9224 7

Printed in China

Franklin Watts is a division of Hachette
Children's Books, an Hachette UK company.
www.hachette.co.uk

Picture credits
Corbis: 5 (Werner Forman), 6 (Gianni Dagli Orti), 8 (Gao
Xueyu/Xinhua Press), 11 (William Manning), 13 (Charles O'Rear),
14 (Ralph White), 16 (Salvador de Sas/ epa), 18 (Walter Bibikow),
22 (Hulton-Deutsch Collection), 23 (Paul Hardy), 25 (Bertrand
Rieger/ Hemis), 27 (G. Bowater), 29 (Atlantide Phototravel),
31 (John Harper), 33 (Gideon Mendel), 37 (Najlah Feanny),
45 (Underwood & Underwood), 47 (Antoine Gyori/ AGP),
49 (Reuters), 50 (Thomas Frey/ dpa).
Science Photo Library: cover (Brian Brake), 39 (David Nunuk),
40 (TRL Ltd), 56 (Henning Dalhoff/ Bonnier Publications),
58 (David A. Hardy, Futures: 50 Years in Space).
Shutterstock: 4 (CROM), 15 (Pieter Janssen), 20 (Richard
Goldberg), 28 (Holger Mette), 35 (Konstantin Sutyagin),
41 (Soundsnaps), 42 (robdigphot).

Cover picture: Robots weld car bodies on an assembly line.

Every attempt has been made to clear copyright. Should there
be any inadvertent omission, please apply to the publisher for
rectification.

CONTENTS

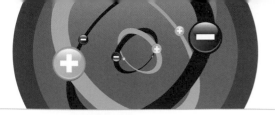

CHAPTER 1

The Progress of Transport

It is hard to imagine life without any form of transport. Yet for most of human history, people have relied on their feet to take them where they needed to go, and on the strength of their muscles to move objects from one place to another.

Wheels with spokes were first used around 2000 BC.

Natural energy

For thousands of years every form of transport relied on the use of natural energy, whether provided by humans, animals or the wind. Asses were probably the first animals to be used to carry heavy loads. The domestication of the horse and the invention of the wheel opened up many new possibilities. Horses could be ridden fast over long distances. They were also widely used in battles to pull wheeled war chariots. The first vessels on water were primitive rafts but, over time, shipbuilding technology developed. Around 3200 BC, the Egyptians began to equip their ships with sails.

Over the centuries, people continued to innovate. Stirrups, bridles and iron horseshoes made riding more efficient, and rudders and compasses on ships improved steering and navigation. Horse-drawn vehicles, from wagons to carriages and coaches, gradually became faster and more comfortable. The construction of

Wheeling forwards

The invention of the wheel was one of the greatest advances in human history. The earliest images of wheeled vehicles, dated around 3500 BC, come from the ancient civilization of Sumeria (in present-day Iraq). These images show solid wooden wheels on war chariots, and on other vehicles that are possibly wagons. Around 2000 BC, lighter, more manoeuvrable wheels with spokes began to appear in the Middle East. Wheeled vehicles have played a huge role in trade and war. Yet the inhabitants of the Americas and Australia did not use wheeled vehicles until they were introduced by Europeans from the sixteenth century onwards.

roads, bridges and canals created better transport links. From the fifteenth century onwards, Europeans learned to build ships that could sail far from land across the oceans. European sailors ventured to America and travelled all round Africa to reach the East by sea.

This artefact, the Royal Standard of Ur, dates from about 2500 BC. Mosaics on this panel depict warriors and chariots. The chariot wheels are filled in – spokes were a later invention.

New kinds of power

In the eighteenth century, wealth, trade and technological progress all combined to produce one of the greatest changes in human history. Britain became the first country to experience the Industrial Revolution. During this time machines took over much of the work that had previously been done by humans and animals. One of the key inventions of the Industrial Revolution was the first efficient steam engine, designed by James Watt in 1769. Since the late eighteenth century, forms of motive (moving) power based on steam, oil and electricity have revolutionized transport.

Steam power

According to legend, James Watt saw steam pouring from the spout of a boiling kettle and realized that he might be able to use the force of steam to drive machines. Watt's steam engines were based on that principle. Coal was burned in a furnace to heat quantities of water. The resulting steam was forced through valves (devices that can open or shut to control the flow of steam) to push pistons (metal rods that move up and down). The up-and-down movement of the pistons worked the engine. The first steam engines were used to drive machinery in mills and factories, but experiments showed that steam could also move vehicles. Within a few years steam engines were being used to power both trains and ships.

This print shows the *Rocket*, George Stephenson's pioneering steam locomotive. It gives an idea of the impact of early trains – the *Rocket* looks like a strange monster in the early nineteenth-century landscape.

The age of oil

On the roads of Europe and America, horse-drawn vehicles crowded the streets until the late nineteenth century. The situation began to change in the 1880s, with the development of the internal combustion engine. Internal combustion means 'inside burning' – this engine ran on a mixture of fuel and air that burned continuously inside a metal tube. This continuous combustion released the energy to push pistons and drive the engine. The internal combustion engine was far more compact than a steam engine, and allowed the development of the motor car.

Car manufacturers soon found that fuels made from oil, such as petrol and diesel, were most suitable for the internal combustion engine. These fuels were soon used to power not only cars but also ships, trains and planes. In this way, oil became the world's most important form of fuel. It remains crucial to the entire global economy, although there are increasing concerns about the effect its use has on the world's environment and climate.

Power at a price

Coal, oil and natural gas are all fossil fuels. Fossils are the remains of plants and creatures that existed hundreds of millions of years ago. Layers of coal and oil represent huge numbers of plants and tiny creatures that have been crushed down by enormous geological pressures into rocks and liquids. Because of their origin as living things, oil and coal consist mainly of carbon, a building block of life – and a vital fuel source for present-day societies. Since fossil fuels were created over many millions of years, they are a non-renewable fuel source. This means they cannot be replaced, and there are fears that within decades there will be none left.

What all the world desires

VIEWPOINT

The Scottish inventor and engineer James Watt went into partnership with a businessman, Matthew Boulton, and opened a factory to manufacture steam engines. Boulton had no doubts about the value of the new technology. In 1776, he told a visitor to the factory:

"I sell here, sir, what all the world desires to have – power!"

Another problem with the use of fossil fuels is that burning them produces pollutant gases. These emissions harm both people and the environment. The constant burning of coal blackened many nineteenth-century cities and is still a significant pollutant in some countries. However, most experts regard oil as the greatest modern pollutant. Emissions from traffic and industry cause chronic air pollution in many cities around the world. For example, air pollution was an issue in 2008 when the Olympic Games were held in Beijing, the capital of China. The Chinese authorities were so concerned about the air quality in Beijing that they halved car traffic until the end of the games. Owners of cars with odd-numbered registrations were allowed to drive only on odd-numbered dates, while drivers with even-numbered registrations were similarly restricted to even-numbered dates.

The use of fossil fuels is also blamed for climate change. Global temperatures are rising, and most scientists believe this is happening because such huge quantities of fossil fuels are being burned. The fuels

Cars on the Second Ring Road in Beijing, the capital of China. Pollution from traffic is a major problem in Beijing.

emit 'greenhouse gases', particularly carbon dioxide (CO_2), which trap heat from the sun in Earth's atmosphere. The predicted consequences of global warming include melting polar ice caps, rising sea levels and increasingly extreme weather conditions.

Electric power

Electricity has important advantages as a form of motive power. Any form of transport powered by electricity is less polluting and quieter than types powered by petrol or diesel. However, other forms of energy are needed to produce electricity. Both coal and oil are burned to generate electricity at power stations, which supply homes, businesses and some types of transport. So, although electricity is clean at the point of use, its production still involves the burning of polluting fuels.

Going electric

Electricity is generated at power stations, so it has to be linked to any type of transport it drives. One method is to transmit electricity through 'live' rails, or overhead wires. Many city transport networks, such as underground (metro) systems and trams, are powered in this way. A large vehicle like a train can carry the necessary fuel, typically diesel, and use it in combination with its own independent generator to produce electricity. Smaller vehicles, such as electric cars, operate by using batteries, which have to be recharged regularly.

PROS: CHANGING TECHNOLOGY

Each new development in transport has allowed people to travel faster and farther. People have been able to explore the world and settle in new regions. Technological change has made global trade and travel possible and has increased human productivity and prosperity.

CONS: CHANGING TECHNOLOGY

Since the late nineteenth century, transport has largely depended on fossil fuels such as coal and oil. Supplies of both are limited. Burning fossil fuels has polluted the environment and is believed to have caused disastrous climate change. Many people believe that the age of oil must end if humanity is to survive.

CHAPTER 2

Water Transport

All through history, water has played a vital role in the transportation of passengers and cargo. Before the arrival of motorized transport, the most efficient way to carry heavy goods (for example, coal from a mine) was along rivers. In some places where there was no river nearby, people dug an artificial waterway, called a canal, to link the place where the goods were produced to the nearest river or port.

Artificial waterways

People have dug canals since ancient times. Construction of the world's longest artificial waterway, the Grand Canal in China, was started as early as the 300s BC. This canal was built to transport grain from the farmlands in the south of China to the cities of the north. In Britain, the heyday of canal building coincided with the Industrial Revolution. A national network of canals was rapidly built to transport coal and goods. In the United States, major projects such as the Erie Canal (which opened in 1825 to connect New York City and Buffalo), became thriving trade routes. Canals became less important for transporting goods as railways and roads developed into faster and more efficient alternatives for freight transport. However, many artificial waterways remain in use today.

Lock gates

Locks are ingenious yet simple devices that allow canals to be built across ground that is not flat. A lock is a short section of a canal with gates at either end. When a boat passes into the lock, the lock gates are shut behind it. Small panels, called sluice gates, in the lock gates are opened to allow water either to pour in or out, depending on whether the boat needs to go up or down. As the water level changes, the boat rises or falls with it. When the water level in the lock is the same as that on the far side of the lock gates, the gates are opened and the boat passes through. In places with steep inclines, a series of locks joined together allows a boat to move smoothly uphill or downhill.

The locks of the Rideau Canal, in Canada, were constructed in the nineteenth century and have been in operation ever since. The canal connects the Canadian cities of Ontario and Kingston.

Ocean-going vessels use ship canals that link inland ports to the sea, or connect two seas or oceans. Some ship canals dramatically reduce the time it takes to complete a voyage. For example, the Suez Canal in Egypt, which opened in 1869, connects the Red Sea to the Mediterranean. Before its construction, ships sailing between the Far East and Europe had to take a route around the southern tip of Africa. Similarly, the Panama Canal in Central America, which opened in 1914, links the Atlantic and Pacific oceans. This 80-km waterway shortens voyages by thousands of kilometres for ships sailing between the east and west coasts of America.

PROS: CANALS

The construction of canals during the Industrial Revolution had a great economic impact, bringing down the cost of transporting heavy goods. Canals also helped to shape local economies. The Erie Canal encouraged settlement of the Great Lakes region. The canal also promoted the growth of New York City by providing an outlet for the goods that came into the United States through its harbour.

CONS: CANALS

Building canals was difficult and dangerous work. Before the introduction of modern engineering techniques and safety precautions, landslides were a constant danger for workers constructing a canal. Canals also dramatically changed the landscape, redirecting natural water sources, and affecting habitats and the environment.

The origins of modern shipping

The history of modern shipping begins with the development of steam-powered ships in the late eighteenth century. Earlier ships had relied on oars and wind power. Steamships were propelled by mechanical engines. As a result they were faster and better able to make their way against winds and currents.

Most early steamships were paddle boats, in which the engine drove a large circular set of paddles either at the back or on the sides of the ship. These paddle steamers were vulnerable in rough seas, because their engines and their large paddle wheels were easily damaged. At first, such ships were fitted with sails in case something went wrong with the engine. Nevertheless, in 1838 one of these paddle steamers, the SS *Sirius*, became the first vessel to cross the Atlantic Ocean, from London to New York, using steam power alone.

In 1843, the first propeller-driven iron ship, the SS *Great Britain*, was launched. A ship's propeller is a spiral of rotating blades that is fully

The paddle steamer *Delta Queen* leaves Natchez, Mississippi, in the American South. From the nineteenth century, paddle boats linked communities up and down the Mississippi river.

submerged in the water at the bottom of the hull. The propeller proved far superior to the paddle wheel for powering ocean-going craft because it was not lifted out of the water by the waves. However, paddle steamers remained in service for some years on inland waterways, most famously transporting passengers and cargo up and down the Mississippi river in the United States.

By the later nineteenth century, steamships were overtaking sailing ships as carriers of cargo all over the world. Improvements to steam engines continued to increase speed and fuel efficiency. From about 1920, the steam was produced by burning the fuel that would dominate future transport – oil.

Submarines

In the seventeenth century, a Dutchman, Cornelius van Drebel, built the first submarine. It was propelled by oars and travelled very close to the surface of the water. A tube poked up into the air so that the people inside could breathe! However, the first effective submarines date from the late nineteenth century. In order for a submarine to dive below the surface of the ocean, large tanks in the ship's hold, called ballast tanks, are filled with water to increase its weight. When it is time to surface again, compressed air is blown into the ballast tanks to force the water out and decrease the vessel's weight.

PROS: STEAMSHIPS

Steamships played a vital role in the expansion of world trade during the nineteenth century. Fleets of merchant ships carried raw materials and mass-produced goods across the globe, while other steamers carried immigrants from Europe across the Atlantic Ocean to settle in the Americas.

 CONS: STEAMSHIPS

People who worked on steamships were poorly paid and their jobs were often dangerous. Many lives were lost at sea. Many accidents happened because vessels were overloaded. In 1875, a British member of parliament, Samuel Plimsoll, championed legislation to restrict how much could be loaded into a ship. As a result, the Merchant Shipping Act of 1876 introduced legal restrictions on the volume of cargo that could be carried. The line on a ship that indicated when the limit had been reached became known as the 'Plimsoll line'.

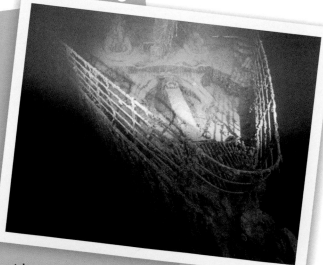

Taken in 1986, this underwater photograph shows the hull of the shipwrecked *Titanic* lying on the seabed, 3,650m below the surface.

Titanic disaster

The *Titanic* was a steamship that was supposed to combine luxury with an engineering design that made it unsinkable. But on its first voyage, in 1912, it hit an iceberg and sank in the Atlantic Ocean. The impact of the iceberg caused a large area of the hull to buckle and water to pour in. The ship's hull was divided into compartments, each of which was supposed to be watertight. However, the barriers between the sections were not high enough. The water destabilized the ship and, as it leant over, water flooded from section to section. The *Titanic* sank rapidly. Of the 2,222 passengers and crew on board, only 705 people survived.

Shipping cargo

Present-day cargo ships face competition from other methods of carrying freight. Yet they continue to take raw materials and finished products to destinations around the world. No rival form of transport can match the volume of cargo they can carry or the price at which they can carry it. Many kinds of cargo are carried in special containers, designed to protect the goods inside. The development in the twentieth century of standard sizes for shipping containers was of particular importance, as it allowed ships to be filled to capacity.

Currently, the largest container ships are those of the Emma Maersk class, measuring 13,500 twenty-foot equivalency units (TEU). This means that these ships can carry up to 13,500 standard containers that measure 20ft (6.1m) by 8ft (2.4m) by 8.5ft (2.6m). Some coastal cities have become centres for the handling and transfer of containers. Examples include Singapore and Shanghai, China, which are two of the busiest ports in the world.

Modern container ships can carry incredible amounts of cargo.

Bulk cargo

Not all cargo is carried in containers. The other main type of cargo, called bulk cargo, is carried loose. Many raw materials including grain, coal and oil are shipped in this way. Oil is transported all around the world in special ships called tankers. Modern oil tankers are enormous, carrying hundreds of thousands of tonnes of oil. Some people object to these

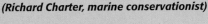

Oil spills

In 2002 the tanker *Prestige* spilled its oil off the coast of Spain, causing extensive environmental damage. Environmentalists again called for an immediate ban on single-hulled oil tankers:

'To permit the use of just one thin single sheet of steel [a single hull] to keep huge volumes of toxic petroleum away from the valuable living marine resources on which our coastal economies depend is an obsolete [out-of-date] transportation strategy. Recent events make it crystal clear that the time has come to accelerate the transition to double-hulled tankers.'

(Richard Charter, marine conservationist)

VIEWPOINT

Cleaning up oil spilt by the tanker *Prestige* in 2002. Only through the painstaking efforts of workers and volunteers can spills such as this be dealt with and environmental damage limited.

supertankers because they can damage the environment if there is an accident at sea. During the twentieth century there were more than 200 recorded incidents involving oil tankers. A well-known example is the *Exxon Valdez*, which in 1989 spilled more than 40 million litres of oil off the coast of the US state of Alaska, causing enormous damage to the wildlife and coastline.

Disasters such as the *Exxon Valdez* accident led to new international agreements to replace single-hulled oil tankers with double-hulled designs. A double-hulled ship has an outer and an inner hull, so any impact would have to break through both hulls before the ship spilled its cargo. From 2010 all oil tankers are supposed to be double-hulled. However, because it is so expensive to replace these enormous ships, many of those in service are of outdated design. Some countries have expressed their intention to allow the continued use of single-hulled oil tankers past the cut-off date.

 PROS: CONTAINER SHIPS AND SUPERTANKERS

Today's methods of carrying cargo are extremely efficient. It is much cheaper to move a single large quantity of freight than to fuel and crew many smaller vessels. These savings are passed on to consumers and help to keep down prices. In the specific case of oil, this efficiency is especially important in view of ever-increasing demand. Shipping can become a central aspect of local economies. Shanghai's busy port has helped it to become the commercial centre of China.

 CONS: CONTAINER SHIPS AND SUPERTANKERS

The huge volume of containers passing through modern ports makes thorough inspection difficult. Most containers are not, in fact, opened. This means that it is hard to prevent smuggling of illegal goods such as drugs, or weapons for use by terrorists. Sometimes, even people are smuggled in containers although, if they are unlucky, they can suffocate while they are inside.

Ferries

Ferries are vessels that regularly transport passengers, and sometimes their vehicles, across bodies of water. In many parts of the world ferries provide vital links to islands, and in some places they form part of a city's public transport. For example, many waterways divide the city of Stockholm, the capital of Sweden, so ferries are a natural means of getting around. Ferries also serve different areas of New York City, and are much-used links between Britain and the European continent.

Many modern ferries are either hovercraft or hydrofoils. Both designs have their hulls lifted out of the water to reduce resistance to their passage. The hovercraft, which came into service in the 1960s, uses

Passengers and vehicles on a ferry to Martha's Vineyard in Massachusetts, United States. Ferries are a vital part of the local transport system in many parts of the world.

powerful fan engines to lift the vessel and create a cushion of air beneath it. The air is contained by a semicircular barrier, called the skirt. Hydrofoils have a wing-shaped structure, called a foil, which lies under the main hull and lifts it above the surface of the water. Only the foil touches the water, its streamlined shape reducing resistance to a minimum.

Ships are used as ferries, in particular for carrying vehicles across bodies of water. These ferries are designed so that passengers can drive straight on to the ship through one end, and off through the other end. These roll-on roll-off ferries are often called ro-ros for short.

Catamarans

The original design of a catamaran – two canoes linked together by wooden poles – comes from Polynesia in the Pacific Ocean. It is remarkably stable even in rough Pacific waters. Western boatbuilders adapted the Polynesian design by turning the canoes into twin hulls. In the 1970s, the catamaran shape was adapted to build ferries. With the hulls reduced to thin blades cutting through the water, and the passenger area carried high above them, catamarans became increasingly streamlined vessels.

 PROS: ROLL-ON ROLL-OFF FERRIES

Ferries provide a convenient way for people to cross short bodies of water. They eliminate the need for plane travel over short distances. Ro-ros also allow people to take their vehicles from one place to another.

 CONS: ROLL-ON ROLL-OFF FERRIES

The ro-ro design has drawbacks. Ro-ro ferries have large entry and exit points for vehicles, and it is vital that these openings are sealed during the voyage. If water does get in, there are few internal bulkheads to prevent it from pouring from side to side along the open space of the vehicle deck. The weight of the water may cause the ship to tip over. This is what happened to the *Herald of Free Enterprise* as it crossed the English Channel in 1987, causing 193 deaths, and to the *Estonia*, which sank in the Baltic Sea in 1994, claiming the lives of 852 people.

Sailing for pleasure

Many people travel by water simply for enjoyment. Recreational sailing is popular on boats ranging from small dinghies to large yachts, and so is canal boating. Speedboats, also called powerboats, are designed to rise up above the water and glide along the surface, allowing them to travel very fast. However, private speedboats can pose an environmental threat. Their rapid passage churns up the water, and can kill off local plant and animal life. This is a major problem in places such as the Everglades, in Florida, United States, where concern for wildlife such as the local manatees has led to increasing restrictions on boating.

Some people like to take their holidays on huge cruise ships, travelling from one place to another. Large ocean liners once dominated passenger transport, for example across the Atlantic Ocean, but they have long since been replaced by planes. Since the 1980s, however, such ships have become popular again for cruising. They are like floating hotels, with luxurious facilities for dining, entertainment and sports.

Luxury cruise ships such as this Caribbean liner are popular because they combine the comforts of a luxury hotel with mobility.

PROS: CRUISE SHIPS

Luxury cruises are popular with many people who want to see the world from a safe base. The tourist trade has become an important source of income for many local economies along cruise routes.

 CONS: CRUISE SHIPS

Infection outbreaks can be a problem on board a cruise ship. Viruses that cause sickness and diarrhoea are easily transmitted between passengers living in a relatively enclosed environment.

Cruise ships release considerable amounts of waste into the sea. Many cruise lines travel similar paths, so their pollution may be harmfully concentrated in specific areas. These ships also take in and release ballast water. This is water contained in the lower hull to stabilize the ship. Ballast water is often brought on board at one place and discharged in another, introducing foreign organisms (living things) that may have a lethal effect on local marine life.

Environmental damage from cruise ships
VIEWPOINT

Studies have shown that cruise ships produce a lot of pollution relative to their small number of passengers:

'Despite the focus on airline emissions, it has become clear that cruise liners are far more polluting per passenger kilometre than planes.'
(Justin Francis, co-founder of Responsibletravel.com)

'the challenge to ferry companies and cruise lines is to protect the environment, minimize negative impacts ... and support sustainable tourism while meeting the increasing demand for travel.'
(Passenger Shipping Association)

CHAPTER 3

Rail Travel

Early in the nineteenth century, the fastest horse-drawn coaches travelled along Britain's roads at an impressive 16kph. But in 1829, when a steam-driven locomotive won a competition in the north of England, it reached a speed of 48kph. The locomotive was the *Rocket* (see page 6), designed by George Stephenson.

By this time, engines run by steam were already performing many tasks, such as pumping water out of mines and driving factory machinery. Engineers had quickly realized that steam power might also be used to drive a wheeled vehicle. Many of them worked on developing a locomotive, a mobile steam engine that could pull a chain of linked wagons or carriages (a train) along a fixed track or railway. There had been a number of more or less successful experiments before Stephenson designed the *Rocket*, but his was the first practical and reliable locomotive.

Steam locomotives

The command centre of a steam locomotive was the cabin, where the driver and fireman worked. The fireman kept the coal in the firebox burning and stoked up. The fire boiled water in a tank that produced steam, which was then forced into cylinders. The pressure of the steam in the cylinder pushed the piston in and out, making the wheels turn. The driver controlled the speed of the locomotive by operating valves that raised or lowered the pressure of steam into and out of the cylinder.

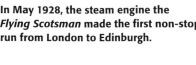

In May 1928, the steam engine the *Flying Scotsman* made the first non-stop run from London to Edinburgh.

Trains and railways were an immediate and spectacular success. By the 1850s, a network of railway lines covered most parts of Britain, and European countries followed suit. The first American railways were constructed in the 1830s. The railways were particularly important in the United States because they linked far-distant places in a vast and still-growing nation. The Union Pacific Railroad was the greatest of several epic American achievements. Completed in 1869, the line stretched across the continent, opening up the American West to new settlements and linking them to settled areas in the east.

Steam maintained its supremacy for many years. In the 1930s, Britain produced record-breaking locomotives such as the *Flying Scotsman* and *Mallard*. In 1938, on an intercity journey in Yorkshire, *Mallard* reached a speed of 202kph, which is still the world record for a steam train. In the United States the most gigantic of all steam locomotives were built in the 1940s. Known as Big Boys, they weighed hundreds of tonnes, were equipped with 16 huge wheels instead of the standard eight, and were up to 40m long. They hauled very heavy loads over long distances, mastered steep inclines and, during World War II (1939–45), transported tanks and other war materials destined for service overseas.

People hurry through a busy railway station in London, UK. Trains provide vital transport links in the twenty-first century.

PROS: THE COMING OF THE RAILWAYS

The railways had a huge impact on economic growth. They were able to carry large amounts of freight at a time when coal and iron were central to economic development. Railways enabled millions of people to travel long distances for the first time and gave others a way to commute between home and work.

CONS: THE COMING OF THE RAILWAYS

Steam locomotives produced significant amounts of soot, which added to the coal-based industrial pollution that lasted until the mid-twentieth century. Rail lines are fixed in place, so other forms of transport are still needed to take people and goods to and from train stations.

Diesel trains

An alternative type of engine that ran on a different fuel, diesel, began to replace steam after 1945. The diesel engine is a form of internal combustion engine that uses hot compressed air to ignite (fire) the fuel. Some trains use a diesel engine to power the wheels directly, while others use it to power an electric generator which drives motors that turn the wheels (diesel-electric). These trains, particularly favoured in the United States and the UK, are therefore powered by electricity without being dependent on an outside electrical source, such as overhead cables.

Diesel-electric trains are easier to maintain but are less fuel-efficient than trains powered directly by diesel engines. Both types are more energy-efficient and cheaper to run than steam trains, and by the 1960s the United States and Europe had gone over to diesel. However, steam trains continue to run in many less economically developed countries.

Burning diesel produces pollutants, including soot and nitrogen oxide, a key ingredient in smog, a fog created by chemical air pollution. Soot and smog have been linked to heart attacks, lung disease and childhood asthma.

Mountain climbing

Conventional trains climb steep inclines by winding gradually upwards around a hillside. Some trains, however, are constructed to go directly up and down a hillside. There are two main ways to prevent trains from slipping on the tracks. A rack-and-pinion railway has a third, toothed rail in the middle of the track, called the rack. The train is fitted with a toothed wheel, the pinion, which interlocks continuously with the rack, ensuring the train's safety. A funicular railway has two separate tracks, each fitted with a continuous loop of strong cable laid between the rails. The cable is attached to a train on each track. As the train at the top moves down, its weight hauls the other train up from the bottom.

Switzerland's Jungfrau railway is the highest in Europe and passes through spectacular alpine scenery. Most of the line operates on the rack-and-pinion principle, in which the train continuously locks in to the 'teeth' of the middle rail.

Electric trains

Many trains are powered directly by electricity. The power for electric trains is supplied either from an overhead cable, or from a third, electrically charged rail that runs beside the tracks. These systems work well for short-distance travel within cities, but the cost of electrifying hundreds or thousands of kilometres of line seemed at first to make them impractical for longer-distance routes. In the late twentieth century, however, rising demand for rail services encouraged new investment in long-distance electric lines. Though electrifying rail tracks is very expensive, once it has been done, electric trains are fast and relatively cheap to run.

At first, long-distance electric trains in Europe generally shared the track with other types of rail traffic. However, electric trains that run on tracks specifically designed for them can go much faster. Japanese engineers were the first to design high-speed electric trains with bullet-shaped ends to minimize air resistance. The tracks were made as straight as possible in the interests of speed. In October 1964, Japan's 'bullet trains' began operating along the first section of the Shinkansen (New Trunk Line), a 515-km stretch between Tokyo and Osaka. From the beginning, Shinkansen trains achieved speeds of up to 210kph. The Shinkansen was progressively extended, and by the twenty-first century, electric trains were travelling all over Japan on high-speed tracks, reaching top speeds of 300kph.

Tilting trains

A bend in a rail track forces conventional trains to slow down and therefore lose time. If a conventional train travels at speed around a bend, the passengers inside feel pushed in the opposite direction and objects slide across the carriage. However, tilting trains can take bends at speed because they have upper sections that lean and so prevent the contents of the carriages from sliding around. The train actually tilts in the same direction as the bend, just as a racing cyclist leans into a corner.

The TGV

Japan still has the fastest regular train services in the world. However, European countries learned from the Japanese example. In 1982, France became the first country in Europe to construct a long-distance line for the exclusive use of high-speed trains. Initially it ran from the capital, Paris, to the southern French city of Lyon. The new type of train was known as the TGV – *train à grande vitesse* (high-speed train). It is so fast that the driver has no time to see ordinary signals. Instead, instructions reach the driver via electric pulses that pass through the rails.

One of France's TGV fleet flashes past a field of sunflowers. First introduced in 1982, the TGVs run at up to 300kph. A number of other countries have introduced similar services.

TGV lines have expanded in France, and the TGV model has been widely adopted by other countries, including Britain. In 1994, the Channel Tunnel, a 51-km-long undersea train tunnel opened. Passenger and freight trains now run under the English Channel on lines that link the British and French rail systems. In Spain, the new Velaro line, from Madrid to Barcelona, opened in February 2008. The Velaro trains average 238kph and can reach speeds of up to 404kph.

Maglev

Magnetic levitation, or maglev, trains use a revolutionary technology that allows them to float above their tracks. A maglev train has no engine or wheels. Instead, it uses electromagnets, powerful magnets operated by an electrical current, to propel itself. Electromagnets are fitted to the bottom of the train and along the tracks, or guideways. The two sets of electromagnets repel each other, lifting the train so that it floats above the guideway. Electromagnetized metal coils on the guideways switch on and off, pushing and pulling the train forward. Because there is no contact between the train and the guideway, and therefore no friction, maglevs are faster, easier to maintain and quieter than any other type of train currently in service.

Maglev technology was developed in Japan and Germany. A maglev train has already broken the TGV's speed record by reaching 581kph. However, the expense of constructing maglev lines has slowed development, and so far the only regular service is in Shanghai, China. If the financial problems can be overcome, the maglev may prove to be the passenger train of the future.

VIEWPOINT

Taking rail to the next level

Many people feel that maglev technology represents the future of fast, environmentally-friendly transport:

'Rail has gone as far as it can go. If you want to take it to the next level, you have to go to maglev.'

(Phyliss Wilkins, chairperson of the US Maglev Coalition)

A maglev train in Shanghai, China, glides along its guideway.

Metro and light rail systems

Moving people around in cities creates special problems for transport planners. All around the world, huge numbers of workers travel between their homes outside the city and their places of work in the city centre. Shoppers and tourists also throng the world's major cities. All these people want fast and efficient transport.

Going underground

In crowded, traffic-jammed streets, one solution is to transport people through tunnels beneath cities. The world's first underground rail line, the Metropolitan Line in London, opened in 1863. The earliest underground trains were steam-driven, but in the 1890s electric trains were introduced. Tracks were laid with three rails. The train wheels ran on two of the rails, while the third, electrically-charged rail supplied the necessary power. The London Underground was followed by underground, or metro, systems in Budapest, Hungary (1896), Boston, United States (1897) and Paris, France (1900). Many more were constructed in the twentieth century, including New York City's subway in 1904.

A train pulls into Tottenham Court Road underground station in central London. Where stations are colourfully decorated and well maintained, travel by underground can be pleasant as well as fast and efficient.

PROS: UNDERGROUND RAIL SYSTEMS

Although they have existed for over 100 years, metro systems remain an efficient way for millions of people to move about big cities without interfering with street life or traffic. Like other electric-based systems, metros give off no polluting emissions. During World War II, London Underground stations also served as bomb shelters, protecting civilians during air raids.

 CONS: UNDERGROUND RAIL SYSTEMS

Tunnelling and underground construction are extremely expensive. That makes underground systems only really worth the cost in big, traffic-jammed cities. Some metro systems are noisy, crowded, hot and often uncomfortable for their passengers.

Light rail systems

The modern tram, or trolley, is a vehicle that carries passengers along rails sunk into city streets. As early as 1853 in Paris, France, horses were used to pull such vehicles. From the 1890s, the vehicles, no longer horse-drawn, were powered by overhead electric wires and competed successfully with motor buses for mass passenger traffic in cities. Some city trains also ran on rails raised above street level. Elevated rail systems, often called 'the El' for short, have been in use in New York City since the 1880s and in Chicago since the 1890s.

As car driving became popular, many people viewed trams on fixed rails as obstructive and outdated. In many cities, noisy trams and trains were scrapped

The light rail solution — VIEWPOINT

Many people are concerned about the problems created by oil-fuelled vehicles. Some argue that the best solution is improved public transport links:

'From an environmental point of view with fuel prices, with climate change, with energy issues, light rail is the answer.'

(Catherine Potter, executive director of the Regional Conservation Council, arguing for a light rail system for the Australian capital, Canberra)

between the 1930s and 1950s. More recently, congestion and pollution from cars has changed attitudes. Many cities have installed updated versions of the tram or some other light rail system. These pass through city centres, often in pedestrian areas where cars are not allowed. They may also act as surface extensions of the underground system. For example, the automated Docklands Light Railway (1987) links the London Underground with the redeveloped areas of East London.

Trains that travel above street level have also made a comeback. Many are monorails, which means they run on a single rail that supplies their electric power. Suspended monorails are particularly spectacular, since they hang below the single rail instead of riding on it.

A smart modern tram on O'Connell Street, the main thoroughfare in the Irish capital, Dublin. Powered by overhead electric cables, trams and other light rail systems are the fastest growing form of city transport.

 PROS: LIGHT RAIL SYSTEMS

Light rail systems are efficient, clean and much cheaper to put in place than new underground lines. They also reduce car use. A survey carried out in St Louis, Missouri, United States, showed that 80 percent of passengers on the city's light rail link preferred it to driving. User-friendly rail systems have helped to revive many run-down city centres.

CONS: LIGHT RAIL SYSTEMS

Some researchers argue that light rail systems reduce road traffic only temporarily and are not worth the considerable expense involved. Light rail routes, unlike bus routes, are permanent and inflexible. If there is a blockage on the tracks, the trains cannot be diverted around it.

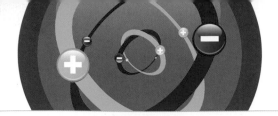

CHAPTER 4

Road Transport

For thousands of years, people have built roads to make it easier to travel from one place to another. However, roads are expensive to construct and maintain. In the past, empire-builders such as the ancient Romans created large-scale road networks. But when empires fell, roads often decayed into rough paths or disappeared altogether. Modern road systems date back no further than the eighteenth century. In the last century, they expanded vastly in the developed world as car travel increased. In much of the less developed world there are still few roads, and most of the population cannot afford to buy cars.

The bicycle

Bicycles became popular in the 1880s, when the first practical models were developed. Today, many countries promote bicycle use for environmental reasons. A bicycle requires no fuel. Its power comes from its rider, who pushes two pedals to turn the wheels via a connecting chain. Cycling gives off no harmful emissions, creates no noise pollution and is great exercise. In parts of the developing world it is the main form of transport.

Mass production

The first engine-powered road vehicles were developed at the beginning of the nineteenth century. They were not very practical, however, as the engines needed a constant supply of fresh coal. The nineteenth century also saw the introduction of vehicles that ran on electricity. They were more successful, but their range was limited. When their batteries ran out, they took hours to recharge. The breakthrough came in the 1880s, when the first motor cars were fitted with internal combustion engines that ran on petrol.

At first motoring was an exciting hobby for the few rather than a revolutionary new mode of transport. The age of the car really began in

1908, when Henry Ford introduced mass-production techniques at his factory in Detroit, United States. Initially, Ford made a single standardized type of car, the Ford Model-T. The Model-Ts were the first widely affordable cars. In the next few decades, other companies followed Ford's example. Competition between manufacturers, along with new technologies, helped to push down prices, allowing more and more people to buy their own cars. Mechanized road transportation developed rapidly, replacing horse riding and horse-drawn vehicles.

The availability of cars has fundamentally affected everyday life in the developed world. Settlement patterns have changed, since people no longer need to be close to the places where they work and shop. They can live in the suburbs or even farther from away from city centres, and drive to work or to the supermarket.

Robotic arms make sparks fly as they work on a car production line in Beijing, China. Advanced methods of mass production helped to make cars widely affordable in the twentieth century. Today, automation makes mass production easier than ever.

PROS: VEHICLES TODAY

Cheap, mass-produced road vehicles have given people freedom of movement. People can travel by car whenever they choose, without being limited to public transport schedules. Many people may prefer to travel in their cars because of the greater comfort, privacy and convenience they offer.

Road vehicles also have great economic importance. Car commuters can travel long distances to work, opening up a wider choice of job opportunities. Businesses can distribute their goods quickly, efficiently and cheaply. Most long-distance cargo spends some part of its journey in a road vehicle. Lorries are not limited to travelling on fixed rails or between ports or airports, so they can carry products and materials from door to door.

CONS: VEHICLES TODAY

The billions of vehicles on the world's roads produce huge amounts of pollution, and the oil that fuels them is a non-renewable resource. In spite of this, many people buy cars which make very inefficient use of fuel. Particularly notorious examples of these vehicles, often described as 'gas guzzlers', are sport utility vehicles (SUVs). The ever-increasing use of the car means that many roads are choked with traffic. The construction of new roads, often undertaken to try to ease congestion, has destroyed large areas of countryside. Other solutions for reducing traffic, such as making drivers pay tolls or charges for using busy roads, are generally unpopular.

Cleaner engines

World demand for oil is enormous. This is partly a result of the tremendous expansion of car use, although other forms of transport also make heavy use of oil products such as petrol and diesel. The Earth's oil reserves are limited, so in the coming decades it will become increasingly difficult to find new supplies of oil. One day, it will all be gone.

Lorries and cars on an interstate highway in the United States. Road links are essential for the delivery of long-distance cargo.

In recent years, many people have accepted that something must be done to reduce our dependence on oil. But not many people are ready to give up the freedom brought by the car. The ideal solution is to replace oil with a different, cleaner, renewable fuel.

Catalytic converters

The development of the catalytic converter was an important advance in reducing emissions from petrol engines. Catalytic converters work by collecting the exhaust fumes produced by the engine and changing their chemical composition. The converters change the poisonous gases nitrous oxide and carbon monoxide into other gases. However, the catalytic converter does not reduce carbon dioxide emissions, so it does not change the contribution made by car use to climate change (see page 8).

At present, one of the most promising alternative technologies is the hybrid car. Hybrid cars use both an internal combustion engine and an electric motor. This is called a dual engine technology. Hybrid vehicles use the electric motor at low power levels and the petrol engine when more power is needed. The electric battery is charged by the motion of the car when it is running on petrol. This means that a hybrid can run mostly off its batteries when moving slowly, for example in busy city traffic, but switches to its internal combustion engine for high-speed driving. Some of the earliest and most successful hybrids were the Toyota Prius, which was first sold in 1997, and the Honda Insight, released in 1999. Today there are a number of hybrid models on the market.

Hybrids use less oil and so produce fewer emissions than ordinary cars. They are not the final solution to oil dependence, as they still use oil and emit pollutants for part of the time. But they are a step in the right direction. The future may belong to cars that do not use internal combustion at all, but instead run on electricity produced by a 'clean' source such as solar power or hydrogen fuel cells (see page 57).

➕ PROS: HYBRID CARS

Hybrid cars burn less oil than conventional cars and produce fewer emissions. Since they use non-polluting electric power when travelling at low speeds, hybrid cars help to reduce the amount of pollution in congested city centres. Hybrid cars also reduce noise pollution, because they are very quiet when running on electric motors. Because they use less fuel, they cost less to run than vehicles that use petrol.

➖ CONS: HYBRID CARS

Hybrid cars are more expensive than conventional cars because their engines are more complicated to make. They need more electrical systems and more batteries than vehicles that run on only one fuel source. Cars have a long operational life, so even if new customers buy hybrids, there will be many old cars on the road for years to come.

A hybrid electric bus travels along Broadway in New York City, United States. Such buses help to reduce polluting emissions and use less fuel than conventional vehicles.

Preparing for life without oil

Many experts argue that we must investigate a range of alternative fuel options:

'No single technology development or alternative fuel can solve the problems of growing transportation fuel use and ... emissions. Progress must come from a comprehensive, coordinated effort to develop and market more efficient vehicles and benign fuels, and to find more sustainable ways to satisfy transportation demands.'

(Massachusetts Institute of Technology report on reducing fuel use and emissions)

Biofuels

Biofuels offer an alternative to fossil fuels. Biofuels are made from carbon extracted from biomass, biological material such as corn, rapeseed, soybeans or sugar cane. Unlike fossil fuels, biofuels are renewable as new crops can be grown each year. Burning biofuels is also 'carbon neutral', meaning that it does not add to the amount of carbon dioxide (CO_2) in the Earth's atmosphere. Burning biofuel does produce CO_2 but it releases the same amount of carbon dioxide that the plant absorbed while it was growing. Though current vehicles do not usually run exclusively on biofuels, many countries are already mixing biofuels in with fossil fuels. Brazil is the largest exporter of a biofuel called ethanol, and is regarded as a world leader in biofuels. Since 1976, ethanol made from sugar cane has, by law, been mixed into all of the petrol sold in Brazil.

VIEWPOINT

The way ahead?

Biofuel production raises both environmental and social issues. Supporters remain optimistic about using it to meet future energy needs. Others warn that, if not carefully managed, it could have negative impacts on people and the environment:

'[Biofuels are] an opportunity to add to the world supply of energy to meet the enormous growing demand and hopefully to mitigate [lessen] some of the price effects [of rising energy costs]. It's an opportunity to do so in an environmentally friendly way and in a way that is carbon-neutral. It's an opportunity to do so in a way that developing countries like Brazil can provide income and employment for their people.'

(Paul Wolfowitz, former president of the World Bank)

'Liquid biofuel production could threaten the availability of adequate food supplies by diverting land and other productive resources away from food crops.'

(United Nations report Sustainable Bioenergy, 2007)

Corn being unloaded for processing into ethanol biofuel at a plant in Iowa, United States. Ethanol production is a controversial issue because it makes use of agricultural land that could be used for food production.

 PROS: BIOFUELS

Mixing some biofuels into petrol and diesel reduces the consumption of these oil-based fuels. The more biofuels are used, the longer the world's supply of oil will last. As fossil fuels become more scarce, biofuels may provide a cheaper alternative.

 CONS: BIOFUELS

Burning biofuels is carbon neutral, but producing biofuels uses a lot of energy. Oil and electricity are needed to grow, harvest, process and transport the biofuel. Biofuel production also requires large areas of land and a supply of water to grow the plants. In some countries, farmers can make more money growing crops for biofuels than food crops. This has led to a drop in the production of some food crops and a rise in world food prices. The increasing demand for biofuels could also be a threat to the world's rainforests. The destruction of rainforests to make room for biofuel crops could accelerate if the demand for biofuels continues.

Safety first

Scientists and engineers have made many technological improvements since the early days of the Ford Model-T. Today, modern cars use a variety of safety systems to limit the severity of a crash. Seat belts began to appear in cars in the 1950s. Seat belts have mechanisms that tighten the belt when it is pulled hard and fast, as it would be during a crash. Fixed to the body of the car, a belt prevents the wearer from being thrown about violently in a collision. Another safety device, the airbag, has been built into some cars since the 1970s. At first these inflatable cushions were installed on the driver's side only, but many modern cars have them for passengers too. If there is a crash, a sensor triggers the airbag to inflate in a fraction of a second. Airbags help to reduce injuries by preventing people from slamming into the hard parts of the vehicle's interior.

Analysis of crash tests helps experts to improve car safety. Using dummies in the tests gives experts an idea of how humans will be affected but avoids putting lives at risk.

Engineers carry out extensive tests to establish the effects of different impacts on the vehicle. They simulate different accidents using dummies in the place of real passengers. This is called crash testing, and it has helped engineers come up with designs that help to protect passengers. For example, the front of many vehicles is designed to crush easily on impact. Called the 'crumple zone', the front of the vehicle operates as a buffer. It cushions the passenger compartment in the event of a crash.

Such safety features have greatly increased the chances of surviving a crash. However, although the percentage of accidents resulting in deaths is down, the overall number of deaths continues to grow as traffic volumes increase.

ABS brakes

Modern cars give the driver improved control over the vehicle, and that can be an advantage in an accident. It takes a wheel less time to stop turning than it takes a moving car to stop. If one wheel locks up when a driver brakes, the car is likely to spin, skid or even flip over. An anti-lock braking system (ABS) prevents any of the wheels on a car from locking up. Computerized sensors on each wheel report the speed of the wheel to the ABS control unit. If a wheel is rotating more slowly than the others, it is beginning to lock up. The ABS system fixes the problem by automatically adjusting the braking pressure on that wheel. With ABS, a driver can steer more effectively while braking hard and the car is less likely to skid or spin out of control.

A car lies on its roof after a road accident. Luckily, the driver survived.

Speeding

Driving above the legal speed limit is a major cause of road accidents. Science and technology have been used to tackle speeding in several ways. Speed cameras are used (particularly widely in the UK) to photograph drivers who break the law, so that police can identify and fine them. Another simple but effective technology is the speed bump. This is a raised section in the road which forces a driver to slow down or risk damage to the car's suspension.

Other new technologies help drivers not to break the law in the first place. Cruise control systems, for example, can be used to maintain a steady speed on long stretches of road. More sophisticated automated systems, called Advanced Driver Assistance Systems (ADAS), help drivers control their cars. Some modern cars are fitted with adaptive cruise control. This system uses lasers or radar to monitor the distance between the car and the vehicle ahead. It slows the car down when it detects the vehicle in front getting too close and speeds up again when it is safe to do so. There are several other types of ADAS, performing tasks ranging from helping drivers find their way to their destinations to detecting that they are falling asleep at the wheel and alerting them.

A hand-held speed camera, one of the modern technologies that help the police to catch drivers who break the speed limit.

PROS: TECHNOLOGY TO THE RESCUE

Studies have consistently shown that safety systems such as seat belts and airbags improve accident survival rates. Technologies that help drivers respect speed limits are also likely to reduce the number of accidents. This approach may be more successful than punishing people by fining them.

 CONS: TECHNOLOGY TO THE RESCUE

Seat belts and airbags do occasionally injure people. Airbags inflate very fast, and can be particularly dangerous to children sitting in the front seat if they hit them in the head. For that reason, young children should sit in the back of a car in correctly fitted booster seats.

Systems such as cruise control reduce the driver's activity, and may cause the driver to lose concentration or fall asleep. Such outcomes could actually cause accidents. Some people think control systems make machines the masters of people. Not everyone trusts computers with their safety.

Driver assistance systems

VIEWPOINT

Many people think that increased automation would significantly reduce car accidents:

'Studies show that at least 93 percent of accidents are caused by human error, so the case for increased driver assistance is clear … By decreasing the driver's workload, detecting dangers and providing the necessary support in hazardous situations, Advanced Driver Assistance Systems (ADAS) could save a considerable number of lives every year.'

(Michael Nielsen, Director for Development and Deployment for the specialist transport group ERTICO–ITS)

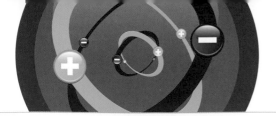

CHAPTER 5

Air Travel

People have long dreamed of travelling through the air. Even ancient myths told stories of individuals who were supposed to have flown, using their arm muscles to move bird-like wings. From the late eighteenth century, aeronauts ('air travellers') rose into the sky in hot-air or gas-filled balloons. A successful attempt to make a heavier-than-air craft took much longer to achieve. Finally, the brothers Orville and Wilbur Wright designed and built a wooden plane with two sets of wings (a biplane). They tested the plane, *Flyer*, on 17 December 1903 at Kitty Hawk, North Carolina, United States. Piloted by Orville, *Flyer* travelled 37m. The flight lasted only 12 seconds, but it began the real conquest of the air.

Within a few years, aviation was headline news. When Louis Blériot made the first flight across the English Channel (1909), people began to realize that flying would change the future of travel. The outbreak of World War I (1914) speeded up technological innovation. Metal was used to build planes instead of wood, and planes with a single set of wings, called monoplanes, began to replace biplanes. Many heroic record-breaking flights were made during the 1920s and 1930s. The most famous was Charles Lindbergh's solo non-stop flight across the Atlantic Ocean from New York to Paris in 1927. Commercial airlines began passenger services, although they were able to carry only a handful of people on each flight. Planes carried some freight, notably

Taking to the air

The design of an aircraft's wings gives the 'lift' needed to rise into the air. The upper surface of the wings is slightly curved and the undersurface is close to flat. When the plane is moving at a sufficient speed, air passing over the curved surface moves more quickly than air passing along the flatter surface. Since fast-moving air exerts less pressure than slow-moving air, the air under the wings pushes upwards, lifting the plane.

post. Mail planes, seaplanes and light aircraft such as those used by 'flying doctors' in Australia, brought many small, remote communities into contact with the wider world.

World War II (1939–45) speeded up advances in aircraft technology. Larger planes were developed to carry troops and huge quantities of freight. These would become models for large passenger airliners and commercial transport planes. The most striking feature of air warfare, however, was the bombing of cities on a scale never seen before. The German 'Blitz' of Britain and the devastating bombing of Germany by the Allies destroyed both military and civilian targets. In August 1945 the United States dropped two atomic bombs that wiped out the Japanese cities of Hiroshima and Nagasaki.

Piloted by Captain Charles Lindbergh, the *Spirit of St Louis* takes off from Roosevelt Field, New York, United States, on 20 May 1927. Lindbergh went on to complete the first solo flight across the Atlantic Ocean, landing at Le Bourget, Paris, on the following day.

PROS: EARLY AIRCRAFT IN PEACE AND WAR

Early feats of aviation were sensational but their impact on peacetime society was limited. However, flights to and from remote communities improved global links in a way that would go on into the twenty-first century. During an international crisis in 1938, the British prime minister, Neville Chamberlain, twice flew to Germany for talks with the German dictator Adolf Hitler. This was an early example of a new kind of leader-to-leader political negotiation that would later become common.

 CONS: EARLY AIRCRAFT IN PEACE AND WAR

Aircraft played an increasingly important role in the two world wars. The suffering of civilian populations under bombing was a new development in the history of war. It meant that conflicts involved entire peoples, not just the armed forces.

The jet age

Work on the jet engine began in the 1930s and continued during World War II. Travelling at over 960kph, even the earliest jets moved twice as fast as propeller-driven planes. After the end of World War II, jet engines were developed to power military aircraft. Then, in 1952, the British company De Havilland put the first jet airliner into service. In 1970, the American company Boeing introduced the 747, the first wide-bodied 'jumbo jet'. It was the world's largest passenger aircraft and would eventually be capable of carrying more than

The jet engine

A jet engine works by sucking in air through its spinning front blades and compressing it so that the air moves with tremendous force. The air passes into a combustion chamber, where liquid fuel is sprayed in. An electric spark ignites the air and fuel mixture. It expands into a burning gas and is blasted out of the nozzle or rear jet. This hurls the plane forwards at an incredible speed. Most modern jet engines, called turbofans, blow air around as well as through the engine. This diminishes engine noise and strengthens the airflow, further increasing the turbofan's power.

400 passengers. In 1974, the European-based Airbus entered service and soon competed strongly with Boeing.

Jet airliners went into service at a time when some countries, for example in North America and Western Europe, were becoming more prosperous. People were able to afford more adventurous holidays, and jet airliners made it possible for many of them to go abroad for the first time. Competition between companies kept prices low. As a result, mass tourism became one of the major industries of modern times.

Many people now believe that the continuing expansion of air travel is having a negative impact on the world. Aircraft engines emit huge quantities of the greenhouse gas carbon dioxide, while emissions of nitrogen oxide cause air pollution around airports. There are also serious problems with noise pollution along flight paths near airports. There are proposals to tax the air travel industry to help pay for the environmental damage it causes. One reason why mass air travel is so popular is that there is no tax on aviation fuel used for international flights. This makes flying cheaper than many other forms of transport. Because of international agreements, this situation is hard to change, although many governments now levy taxes on tickets and flights.

An Airbus 380 comes in to land at the Paris Air Show in 2007. This huge aircraft can carry up to 500 people in great comfort. First-class passengers enjoy luxuries such as private apartments and business meeting rooms.

PROS: MASS AIR TRAVEL

Large numbers of people now enjoy experiences that formerly only the rich could afford. Tourism stimulates the world economy and brings money and employment to poor countries visited by wealthy tourists. Air travel has helped many businesses expand globally. Businesspeople routinely fly to corporate offices all over the world for meetings and to check in on their operations in other countries.

 CONS: MASS AIR TRAVEL

Planes are among the worst polluters, responsible for more than half the environmental damage done by all forms of transport. Low aviation taxes are unfair to competing forms of transport, including more environmentally friendly services such as trains. Worldwide air travel has also had an impact on health. Travellers who move rapidly from one continent to another can spread infectious diseases with frightening speed. This happened in 2003, when SARS (severe acute respiratory syndrome) spread within a few months from China to places all over the world.

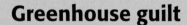

VIEWPOINT

Greenhouse guilt

Environmental organizations such as Friends of the Earth are critical of UK policies on climate change and the role of aviation. In 2007, a spokesperson declared that:

'Aviation is the fastest growing source of carbon dioxide in the UK. Emissions have more than doubled since 1990. The government must ensure the cost of flying reflects the environmental damage aviation causes. And it should abandon plans to allow new runways to be built.'

(Mike Childs, Senior Campaigner, Friends of the Earth)

Supersonic flight

Flight is supersonic when it is faster than the speed at which sound travels (about 1,255kph). When an aircraft reaches that speed, it is said to have broken the sound barrier. Supersonic military jets began flying in 1947. Britain and France cooperated to produce Concorde, which in 1976 became the first supersonic passenger airliner to go into regular service. With its beak-like nose and wings, Concorde became famous all over the world. Cruising at an average speed of 2,150kph, Concorde could carry 100 passengers from New York to London in just three-and-a-half hours. That is half the time it takes a normal jet to cross the Atlantic Ocean. Concorde broke many speed records before being retired in 2003. Because of their great expense, no more supersonic airliners have since been built.

Passengers wear masks on a 2003 flight from Manilla, in the Philippines, to Singapore. The masks are protection against SARS, a dangerous flu-like illness that was carried by air travellers and rapidly spread across the world.

An Antonov An-225 cargo plane takes off from Frankfurt-Hahn Airport, Germany. The world's largest operational aircraft, the six-engined Russian Antonov was originally designed to carry parts for the Soviet space programme.

Transporting cargo by air

Most passenger aircraft carry some freight but much greater amounts are transported by specialized cargo planes. Since the 1960s, consumers in prosperous countries have bought goods that are manufactured or produced abroad, often on other

Space transport

Space vehicles are probably the most exclusive forms of transport. In 1961, Yuri Gagarin, a Russian, became the first person in space, orbiting Earth in *Vostok 1*. Yet even now, only about 500 people have gone into space. They include the teams of the US Apollo missions, which culminated in the landing of *Apollo 11* on the Moon in 1969. Early rocket-powered spacecraft could be used only once. Today, astronauts travel to and from the International Space Station aboard the space shuttle. The shuttle is designed to land like an aeroplane and can be reused again and again.

continents. This globalization of trade means that many goods are transported thousands of kilometres across the world to be sold. In wealthy countries, many consumers have acquired a taste for exotic or out-of-season foods. Air transport is a good way to carry perishable foodstuffs, such as fruits and fish, because it is much faster than sea or road transport.

The cargo plane has become a specialized aircraft. It is big-bodied, with wings and tail mounted high to make loading and unloading cargoes as easy as possible. Cargo planes can carry heavy loads, but supercargo planes have an astonishing capacity. The largest supercargo of all is the gigantic, six-engined Antonov An-225, which can fly up to 800kph and carry cargo weighing up to 250,000kg. It can hold another plane, or a locomotive, but on its first commercial flight, in 2002, it transported 216,000 prepared meals from Stuttgart, Germany, to Oman for US military personnel!

 PROS: AIR FREIGHT

The goods transported by cargo planes offer people a wider range of things to buy. Cargo planes make it possible for fresh produce to be exported to countries all over the world. This benefits the global economy and increases trade opportunities between poor and rich countries. When a disaster occurs, cargo planes can bring emergency medical and food supplies to remote places.

 CONS: AIR FREIGHT

Like passenger aircraft, freight planes are a major source of pollution. This may prove to be too high an environmental price to pay for the luxury of transporting exotic foods around the world. Globalization has significant disadvantages. In practice, many food-producing countries have specialized in growing particular crops to supply wealthy countries, and then found themselves at the mercy of changes in demand.

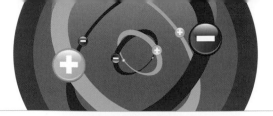

CHAPTER 6

The Future of Transport

It is hard to predict what transport will be like in the far future. No one can be certain what forms the next great breakthroughs will take. Some people believe there will be intergalactic spacecraft and energy beams that instantly transport a person from one place to another. These remain science fiction, at least for the time being. But new developments in water, rail, road and air travel may be just around the corner.

Faster sea travel

Despite the role played by supertankers, sea travel is less important today than it was a century ago. Slower than aircraft and less convenient than cars, ships face stiff competition. But future innovations in water transport could change the situation.

New technologies may enable engineers to build much faster seafaring vehicles. One example is the supersonic submarine. Scientists and engineers have already broken the underwater sound barrier using small test models. No one has built an operational supersonic submarine yet, but such a vessel could potentially achieve incredible speeds – thanks to a bubble of gas!

The key to this technology is to insulate the object from the water around it. Water is

Air lubrication

Under development by the Maritime Research Institute Netherlands (MARIN), air lubrication seems likely to be widely used long before the supersonic submarine. The idea is similar – to create a layer of gas between the hull of the ship and the water, reducing friction between the two. Researchers have had some success testing this method on small model craft, but it has yet to be tried on full-size ships. Air lubrication could substantially reduce the fuel consumption, and therefore the running costs and environmental impact, of seafaring.

much denser than air, so it produces far more resistance to the progress of a craft. Insulating a submarine by surrounding it with a gas bubble reduces resistance and allows the craft to move faster. However, scientists have not yet found a way to sustain supersonic speeds over a long period undersea. Propelling a full-size supersonic submarine would require a great deal of thrust. Existing engines that are powerful enough for the task are too big and heavy to be fitted into a submarine. If engineers overcome these difficulties, the supersonic submarine could have a promising future.

Submarine

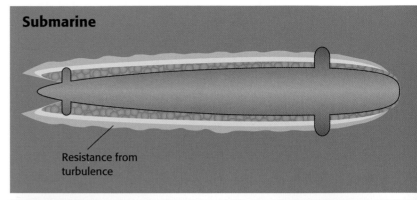

Resistance from turbulence

Supersonic submarine

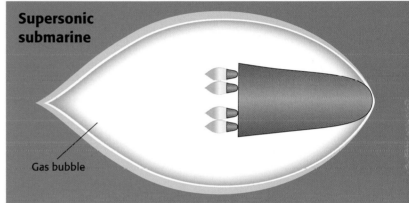

Gas bubble

 PROS: SUPERSONIC SUBMARINE

Undersea travel could provide low-cost and low-pollution transportation. It could also reduce people's current dependence on air travel. In the future, perhaps, people will go to their holiday destinations aboard supersonic submarines.

 CONS: SUPERSONIC SUBMARINE

Opening up the undersea environment to increased human travel could have an unfavourable impact on marine life. A submarine may discharge pollutants into the surrounding water. The high-speed passage of a supersonic submarine might also have unforeseen effects on underwater life.

This artist's impression contrasts a normal submarine (top) with a supersonic submarine surrounded by a bubble of gas. The bubble does away with the drag caused by the contact between the water and the submarine's surface, which slows down present-day vessels.

Flying trains

The Kohama Laboratory at Tohoku University, Japan, is working on a new transport technology that merges air and rail travel, the aero-train. It hovers about a centimetre above its track, held up by a cushion of air. The train has L-shaped wings, which allow it to ride on a pocket of high-pressure air within a walled track. The aero-train's greatest advantage is its low energy consumption. It should be an entirely clean form of rail transport, running on solar and wind power. The designers hope to have a full-scale train, capable of travelling at up to 350kph, running by 2020.

The aero-train will have a walled track to allow it to fly along a pocket of trapped air. It will be powered entirely by clean sources, including wind power captured by turbines.

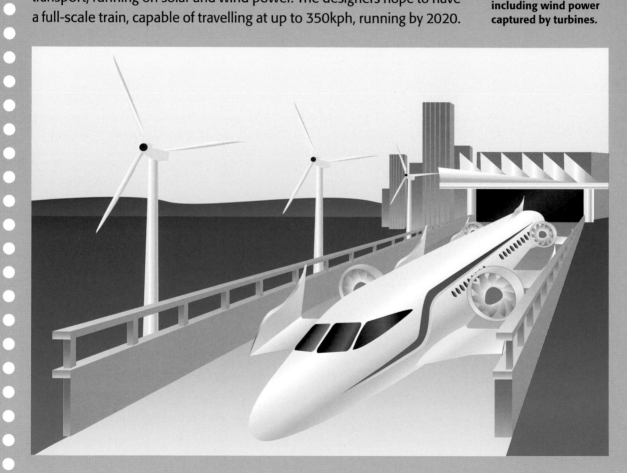

High-tech railways

Some modern trains are already impressively fast but new technology could raise speeds even further. One idea for the future is the vacuum tube train. The air around us on Earth contains molecules of gas but they are not present in a vacuum – it is completely empty space. This means that an object can travel at extremely high speeds through a vacuum because there is no air resistance.

Vacuum tube trains would work on the maglev principle (page 28). But as well as hovering above magnetized rails, they would travel through a system of large tubes. The air would be sucked out to create a vacuum inside the tubes, allowing the train to travel through them at incredible speeds. Engineers think that a vacuum tube train might achieve speeds as fast as 3,200kph. The trains would be designed so that cars could be driven on to them at local stations. One idea is to construct a submerged floating tube 45 to 90 metres beneath the Atlantic Ocean, anchored at intervals to the ocean bed. Trains inside the tube would be able to cover the distance between the United States and Europe in only an hour. With a worldwide network of vacuum tubes, travelling around the planet could become an amazingly simple matter.

 PROS: VACUUM TUBE TRAINS

Vacuum tube trains could provide fast transportation around the world. They would run on electricity, preferably generated using clean technologies. This could lead to a reduction in pollution by reducing the number of air and road journeys. If people were able to drive their cars on to the vacuum tube train, they could travel conveniently to and from stations. By taking the train for part of the trip, they would make their journey faster and create less pollution.

 CONS: VACUUM TUBE TRAINS

Building a network of vacuum tubes would be hugely expensive. It would require a massive investment by private companies or nations. People would probably object to the ugliness of giant tubes unless they were built underground or along the seabed. Wherever the tubes were located, clearing a path for them would have a powerful and probably undesirable impact on the natural environment.

Many people have tried to develop **flying cars**. This artist's impression shows the Moller Skycar, which has been in development since the 1960s. How well it will perform is still not fully known.

Fuelling the future

For the last two centuries, the main forms of transport have depended on burning fossil fuels. But now the threat of climate change and the eventual exhaustion of oil reserves make it vital for people to develop different, sustainable energy sources.

Electricity could become an unlimited source of power for cars. Today, electric cars have a limited range because their batteries soon run out and take a long time to

Flying cars

Cars that can fly seem like a sci-fi dream that would make traffic jams a thing of the past! However, a British company, Parajet, has developed the Skycar, a buggy fitted with an unfolding wing which drivers can deploy when they wish to take to the skies. A powerful rear fan provides the lift that carries the Skycar up and away, at speeds of up to 130kph. Even so, it could be some years before most of us are capable of travelling to work or school in our flying cars!

recharge. Using hydrogen fuel cells would be one way of solving this problem. The hydrogen is extracted from water in a process called electrolysis, and used to power hydrogen fuel cells. A hydrogen vehicle can use this fuel to produce electricity by converting the hydrogen back into water. Instead of being plugged in for hours to recharge its batteries, a hydrogen vehicle can refill at a hydrogen fuelling station. Some hydrogen cars and fuelling stations already exist, but the technology is not yet widely available. It remains to be seen whether this or other alternatives will power the cars of the future.

 PROS: HYDROGEN CARS

Hydrogen cars may be the solution to the problems of twenty-first century road transport. Hydrogen is produced from water, which is far more abundant than the oil used to produce petrol. The water is not lost in the process, but re-formed as a by-product of releasing the energy from the hydrogen. The process of generating electricity from a hydrogen cell also produces no pollution. The car's only emission is water vapour.

 CONS: HYDROGEN CARS

If hydrogen-fuelled cars became the norm, a vast and expensive network of hydrogen refuelling stations would have to be constructed. Vehicles that burn hydrogen do not produce pollutants, but they are only environmentally friendly if the hydrogen fuel cells are manufactured in a clean way. To make the fuel cells, electricity is used to extract hydrogen from water. But much of today's electricity is produced by burning fossil fuels, the resources we hope to do without! To be a real advance, the fuel cells for hydrogen vehicles would have to be manufactured using alternative sources of electricity such as nuclear, wind or solar power. It might in fact be better to focus on improving battery design, so that cars can run directly on electricity rather than making it from hydrogen.

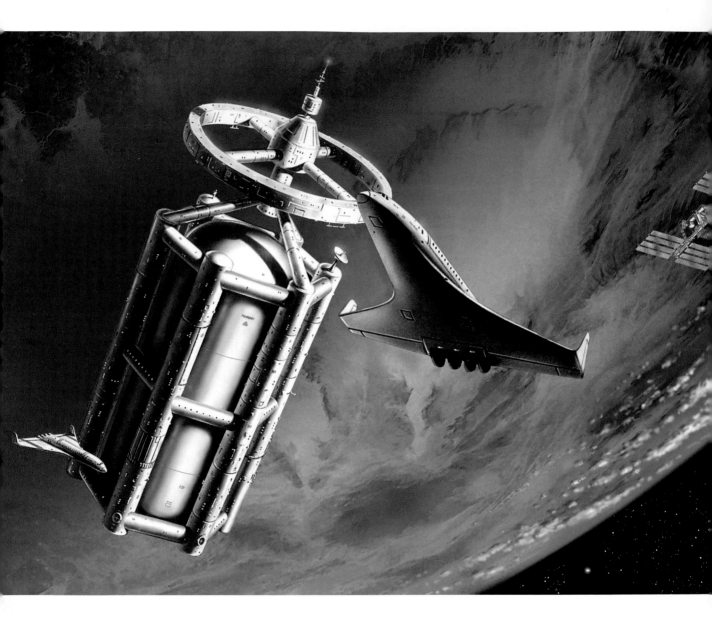

This illustration shows two passenger shuttles docking with a space hotel, with the International Space Station visible in the distance. This kind of space tourism might become common during the twenty-first century.

Transport above and beyond

The future will bring faster, better and cleaner versions of existing forms of transport: new ships, trains, cars and planes. But it may also radically change where and how we travel. A limited number of individuals – mostly scientists and highly trained astronauts – have already travelled into space, reaching as far as the Moon. However, services offering to take paying customers up into space are already running. This 'space tourism' may prove to be the beginning of mass travel, or even settlement, in space.

 PROS: SPACE PLANES

Travelling into space could mark the beginning of a new era for humanity. Astronauts have described how wonderful it is to see Earth from space. In the near future, many more people may experience this. Space transportation could open up new possibilities for the human race, such as the colonization of other planets and the mining of the resources of moons and asteroids.

 CONS: SPACE PLANES

Regular launches of space planes into orbit involve burning quantities of fuel, damaging the environment. Future technologies may help to minimize the damage, but travelling into space is likely to remain very expensive in terms of money and resources.

Future of transport

VIEWPOINT

Everyone seems to be worried about pollution, congestion and the exhaustion of fossil fuels. But some people are optimistic about the future of transport:

'In a relatively short period of time – maybe 15 to 20 years – I believe we're going to fly hypersonic [more than five times faster than the speed of sound]… Travel time may be reduced to as little as 60 minutes anywhere on Earth.'

(Burt Rutan, aerospace engineer and designer of the first privately-developed crewed vessel to reach space, SpaceShipOne)

GLOSSARY

ass A member of the horse family, also known as a donkey.

aviation The art and science of flying aircraft.

ballast tank A tank on a boat or ship that is filled with water to help keep the craft stable. In submarines, the ballast tank is filled or emptied to allow the vessel to rise or dive.

ballast water The water used to fill a ballast tank.

biofuel Fuel made from biomass, usually plants.

biomass Biological (organic) matter such as plants or animals.

bulk cargo Cargo, usually raw materials or foodstuffs, that is carried loose.

bulkhead A partition on a boat, separating different sections.

carbon A non-metallic chemical element that combines with other elements to form the basis of living organisms.

carbon neutral Not emitting carbon, or compensating for carbon emitted by absorbing an equal amount of carbon.

cargo Goods carried by commercial transport.

catamaran A vessel with two hulls.

climate change This could describe any change in climate, but in current use it means the changes believed to be taking place in the world's climate as a result of burning fossil fuels.

compressed Describes a substance that has been pressed or squeezed so that it occupies less space than in its natural state.

container ship A ship designed to carry cargo in standard-sized containers.

crash test A test carried out on a vehicle, using dummies instead of human passengers, that is designed to establish the effect of different impacts on the vehicle.

cruise control An automated system that controls the speed at which a vehicle moves.

crumple zone The front part of a vehicle that is designed to cushion the passenger compartment in the event of a crash.

domesticate To adapt a plant or animal so that humans can make use of it.

double hulled Describes a ship with an inner and an outer hull.

electrolysis The passing of electricity through a liquid in order to separate it into its component parts. For example, it can be used to separate water (hydrogen oxide) into hydrogen and oxygen.

electromagnet A magnet that produces a magnetic field only when an electric current is passed through it.

emission Gas that is sent out or discharged when fossil fuels are burned; more widely, any gas, fluid or heat that is given off.

fossil fuel A fuel that is made up of the decomposed remains of plant and animals. The main fossil fuels are oil, natural gas and coal.

GLOSSARY

freight Goods carried by commercial transport.

friction The resistance caused by the rubbing together of two objects that are in contact and which can slow down vehicles; for example, friction between the wheels and the tracks slows down a train.

fuel cell A mechanism that produces energy by combining elements to create a reaction. In most fuel cells hydrogen is combined with oxygen to release energy and water.

funicular A type of mountain railway with two cars attached to a continous loop of cable. The weight of the downward car pulls the other car up the mountain.

generator A device for generating electricity.

global warming The process by which the average temperatures of the near-Earth atmosphere and Earth's surface are gradually rising.

greenhouse gas Any gas that contributes to climate change by retaining heat from the sun in the Earth's atmosphere.

hovercraft A craft, usually used as a ferry, that moves above water on a cushion of air.

hull The main body of a vessel.

hybrid Something that combines two different types of things. A hybrid car, for example, runs on two different power sources.

hydrofoil A craft that moves above water, carried by a streamlined, wing-shaped structure, called a foil.

Industrial Revolution A period that began in the late eighteenth century in Britain in which there was rapid development of industrial technology and the use of energy from fossil fuels.

internal combustion engine The type of engine used in cars, based on continuous combustion (burning) of petrol.

lock On a canal, an ingenious device that allows boats to move up or down from one level to another.

locomotive The engine used to draw a train along a track.

maglev A high-speed train, raised in the air by magnetism so that it 'floats' above the rails.

mass production An industrial technique by which goods are produced in huge quantities through standardization, each item being identical.

merchant ship A ship used in commerce.

navigation The art and science of planning and following a route to reach a specific destination.

paddle boat A boat that is propelled by paddle wheels, either at the back or on each side.

petrol A form of fuel made from oil and used in internal combustion engines.

piston A movable rod or disc in steam and other engines.

Plimsoll line The line on the hull of a ship that indicates how low in the water it can sit, and therefore the maximum load for that ship.

GLOSSARY

propeller A device with blades radiating from a hub. The thrust produced when the blades turn can propel a ship or an aircraft.

rack-and-pinion Describes a type of mountain railway in which a toothed wheel (the pinion) continuously locks the train to a central toothed rail (the rack).

road haulage Carrying goods by road.

roll-on roll-off (ro-ro) A type of ferry with doors at either end to allow vehicles to drive on and off in the same direction.

sensor A device that detects changes in its environment. Sensors can be set to trigger other systems, for example inflating an airbag when they register a car crash.

ship canal A canal that links two seas or oceans, or one that links a port to the coast. Such canals are usually big enough to allow the passage of large ships.

single hulled Describes a ship with one hull.

sluice gate In the lock gate of a canal, a small panel that allows water to enter or leave the lock.

smog A chemical fog.

smuggle To import or export something illegally and secretly.

solar power Energy from the sun.

soot Powdery black matter, deposited on surroundings after substances such as coal have been burned.

spoke On a wheel, one of the bars that connects the hub (centre) and the rim, holding the rim firmly in place.

supersonic Faster than the speed of sound (about 1,255kph).

TGV (*train à grande vitesse*) One of the fleet of high-speed trains that forms part of the rail network in France.

thrust A force that produces motion, for example from the movement of a propeller.

vacuum Empty space containing no matter, not even air.

valve A device that regulates the flow of gas or liquid in machinery by opening or shutting.

wind power Energy produced by harnessing the force of the wind.

FURTHER INFORMATION

WEBSITES

http://www.transitpeople.org/lesson/trancovr.htm
The TransitPeople's Transportation Lessons site covers transport history, gives information about trains, examines some of the problems caused by cars and describes different modes of public transport. It includes online quizzes.

http://www.ecokids.ca/pub/eco_info/topics/environmental/errandRun/index.cfm
From the EcoKids site, this interactive game shows how alternative methods of transport can help protect the environment.

http://www.faa.gov/education/educator_resources/educators_corner/index.cfm?item=kid
The US Federal Aviation Administration site for children includes activity items such as colouring books, word puzzles and experiments based on the history and future of aeroplanes.

http://www.transport-pf.or.jp/english/index.html
The Transport in Japan site has information about Japanese transport history and vehicles of all kinds. It includes a game and quiz.

BOOKS

Machines at Work: Aeroplane
Caroline Bingham, Dorling Kindersley (2003)

Go! The Whole World of Transportation
Samone Bos, Phil Hunt and Andrea Mills, Dorling Kindersley (2006)

21st Century Debates: Transportation
Rob Bowden, Wayland (2004)

Designed for Success: Superboats
Ian Graham, Heinemann (2008)

Mighty Machines: Aircraft
Ian Graham, Watts (2009)

The Cutting Edge: Transportation – High Speed, Power and Performance
Mark Morris, Heinemann (2006)

Illustrated Science Encyclopedia: Transport
Chris Oxlade, Lorenz Books (2003)

Mighty Machines: Trains
Chris Oxlade, Watts (2009)

Machines Rule!: On the Road
Steve Parker, Watts (2008)

Ocean Liners
Karl Zimmermann, Boyds Mills Press (2009)

INDEX

Page numbers in **BOLD** refer to illustrations and charts.